FROM FARM TO DINNER TABLE

Food's Great Journey

by Doris Licameli

Table of Contents

Introduction

It's dinnertime! Dad has cooked a meal for us tonight. This one looks and smells like it could be a masterpiece. Later, there will be a magnificent apple pie for dessert. Dad's meals have become a tasty tradition in our house. All the ingredients in his recipes are **fresh**.

Eating fresh foods is important. We need the **vitamins** in these foods to keep us healthy. Where do these fresh foods come from? How do the foods on our dinner table make it to our local stores?

↻ Fresh foods have the vitamins our bodies need to stay healthy.

Chapter 1 On the Farm

People all around the world get their food from farms. Farmers plant crops like fruit, vegetables, and grains. Then they **harvest** them when they are ripe. **Livestock**, such as chickens and cattle, is raised on farms to be sold. Chickens are raised for their eggs and meat. Cattle are raised for meat and milk.

The United States has thousands of farms. Different foods are grown in many different areas. These foods then travel from farms to stores all over the country.

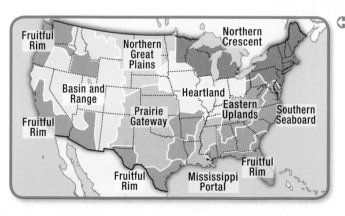

C This map shows the farm areas throughout the United States where different foods are grown.

FAST FACT There are about 77,000 farms in Wisconsin alone. Each farm provides food for 135 people.

⋒ Local farmers often sell their fruits and vegetables themselves.

In the past, travel took much longer than it does now. Horses pulled wagons over bumpy dirt trails instead of paved roads. Food would go bad from the time it went from the farm to the store. People had to eat food that was grown locally. Many people grew their own food to eat.

The Apple Man

Early settlers brought apples to North America. Later, Native Americans planted apple trees. John Chapman helped spread apple trees across the country. He planted apple seeds wherever he went. He is now known as "Johnny Appleseed."

Then things began to change. People moved to new places across the country. They needed goods and services. Better roads were built to connect towns and cities. Railroad trains and steamboats also connected places. Goods could now be shipped all over the country.

In 1869, the first ➲ transcontinental rail line was completed at Promontory Point, Utah.

⋒ Steamboats are still used today to ship food to many parts of the world.

Chapter 2 Trucks On the Job

In the early 1900s, motor trucks replaced slow, horse-drawn wagons. Now food was delivered a bit faster than before. But the trucks broke down often. They had no doors or roofs, so food could not be delivered in the rain or snow.

↑ Most early trucks didn't have headlights to see in the dark. Drivers used oil lamps to see at night.

FAST FACT

In 1916, it took 31 days for a truck to travel from Seattle to New York City. Today that same trip would take about 5 days.

⌒ Refrigerated trucks ▸ .... ⌐bles, and meat at the right ten......

Today highways co........ ....f the country. Modern food d....... are huge **refrigerators** on wheels. Some have 18 wheels. In these trucks, all kinds of food stay fresh throughout the trip. They travel from farms to factories and then to stores without spoiling.

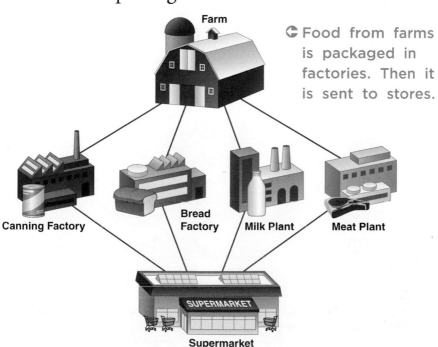

Farm

Canning Factory

Bread Factory

Milk Plant

Meat Plant

Supermarket

↺ Food from farms is packaged in factories. Then it is sent to stores.

Chapter 3 Trains, Ships, Planes

Imagine how happy farmers must have been when steam locomotives were invented in the 1800s. The first trains could go 20 miles (32 km) per hour. They could bring food across the country in a week instead of a month. And these new trains could hold more pounds of food than trucks could. Livestock, grain, and other heavy goods could travel from farms to stores. People could now buy fruits and vegetables all year long.

Miles of Freight	
A ton-mile is one ton carried one mile. One ton is 2,000 pounds (907 kg).	
Year	**Ton-miles of Freight Carried**
1860	3 billion
1900	141 billion
2002	$1\frac{1}{2}$ trillion

Label It

Labels on fresh and canned food helped shippers know what they were shipping. They also helped people see where the food was grown.

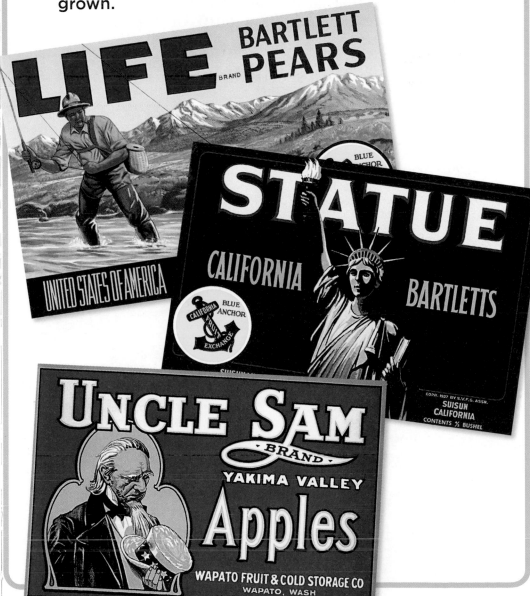

Ships were also used to move food. A shipping container is a big metal box, usually 20 feet (6 m) long and 8 feet (2$\frac{2}{5}$ m) wide. Each one holds a huge amount of goods. Each container is filled and then moved from a truck to a ship or train. As it is moved, it does not have to be opened or repacked. This speeds up the loading and unloading of ships and trains.

⬆ Shipping containers can be loaded and unloaded from freight trains quickly.

FAST FACT   There can be as many as 5,000 containers on a single ship.

Shipping containers can be stacked like blocks on the deck of a ship. Large cranes load and unload them. The containers are refrigerated to keep food fresh. This requires power, so they are stored close to electric outlets on ships.

⊍ Shipping containers lock into place when they are stacked on top of each other.

The Banana Boat

In the late 1890s ships carrying bananas were painted white. It was thought that white would reflect the hot sun and keep the bananas at the tropical temperature they were used to. These ships were called the Great White Fleet.

Airplanes also move food quickly and safely. Airplanes fly hundreds of miles an hour. Shipping by air costs more than by land, so not all foods are shipped by air. Pineapples must be shipped as soon as they are picked so they will stay ripe. They are flown from South America and rushed on trucks to **markets** around the world.

FAST FACT Four cents of every dollar spent on food goes for transportation.

Fresh fish and other seafood are also shipped on planes. Some seafood is caught in the ocean and shipped to restaurants and markets the same day.

⬇ Fresh fish markets receive daily shipments containing thousands of pounds of fish.

Conclusion

Since most people don't live on farms, the best way to get fresh farm food is to ship it quickly. Food can keep its vitamins when it reaches markets quickly. Then we can have fresh food from around the world all year long.

Now people are looking for new ways to deliver food quickly and easily. How do you think people will get food from the farm to your dinner table in the future?

↺ What kinds of food do your local farmers grow?

Progress in Travel		
		Propeller Airplane **1903**
1800		**1900**
1807 Steamboat	**1829** Steam Locomotive	**1892** Gasoline Auto

Glossary

fresh *(FRESH)* newly done, made, or gathered *(page 2)*

harvest *(HAHR-vist)* the gathering in of a crop when it is ripe *(page 3)*

livestock *(LIGHV-stahk)* farm animals used to sell or trade as goods *(page 3)*

market *(MAHR-kit)* a place where goods are sold *(page 12)*

refrigerator *(ri-FRIJ-uh-ray-tuhr)* an appliance, box, or room with a cooling system, used to keep food from spoiling *(page 7)*

vitamin *(VIGH-tuh-min)* one of a group of substances needed in small amounts for the health and the normal working of the body *(page 2)*

Index

Comprehension Check

Summarize

Compare and contrast the way food is moved by trucks with the way food is moved by airplanes. Use a Venn diagram to record your answers. Then use the diagram to summarize the book.

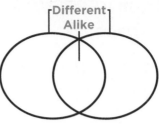

Think and Compare

1. Reread pages 6–7. How have food trucks changed over time? *(Compare and Contrast)*

2. What are some of your favorite meals and recipes? Why do you like them? *(Evaluate)*

3. How do you think the lack of rain on farms can make the cost of some foods go up? *(Synthesize)*